ANGELS OF BATAAN AND CORREGIDOR

The Heroic Nurses of WORLD WAR II

by Agnieszka Biskup   illustrated by Samantha F. Chow

CAPSTONE PRESS
a capstone imprint

Published by Capstone Press, an imprint of Capstone.
1710 Roe Crest Drive, North Mankato, Minnesota 56003
capstonepub.com

Library of Congress Cataloging-in-Publication Data
Names: Biskup, Agnieszka, author. | Chow, Samantha Feriolla, illustrator.
Title: Angels of Bataan and Corregidor : the heroic nurses of World War II / by Agnieszka Biskup ; illustrated by Samantha Feriolla Chow
Other titles: Heroic nurses of World War II
Description: North Mankato, Minnesota : Capstone Press, an imprint of Capstone, 2022. | Series: Graphic library: Women warriors of World War II | Includes bibliographical references. | Audience: Ages 8–11 | Audience: Grades 4–6 | Summary: "Soon after the Japanese attacked Pearl Harbor on December 7, 1941, they also attacked U.S. military installations in the Philippines. For the army and navy nurses stationed there, what had been a peaceful outpost quickly turned into a raging war zone. When the U.S. and Philippine forces retreated to the Bataan Peninsula and the fortress island of Corregidor, the nurses followed them to the field hospitals to care for the wounded. Persevering through enemy assault and imprisonment, these heroic women became angels of mercy amid the war in the Pacific"—Provided by publisher.
Identifiers: LCCN 2022005380 (print) | LCCN 2022005381 (ebook) | ISBN 9781666333916 (hardcover) | ISBN 9781666333978 (paperback) | ISBN 9781666333923 (pdf) | ISBN 9781666333947 (kindle edition)
Subjects: LCSH: World War, 1939–1945—Prisoners and prisons, Japanese—Juvenile literature. | Prisoners of war—Philippines—Juvenile literature. | Prisoners of war—United States—Juvenile literature. | World War, 1939–1945—Participation, Female—Juvenile literature. | United States—Armed Forces—Nurses—Juvenile literature. | World War, 1939–1945—Campaigns—Philippines—Bataan (Province)—Juvenile literature. | World War, 1939–1945—Campaigns—Philippines—Corregidor Island—Juvenile literature. | World War, 1939–1945—Prisoners and prisons, Japanese—Comic books, strips, etc. | Prisoners of war—Philippines—Comic books, strips, etc. | Prisoners of war—United States—Comic books, strips, etc. | World War, 1939–1945—Participation, Female—Comic books, strips, etc. | United States—Armed Forces—Nurses—Comic books, strips, etc. | World War, 1939–1945—Campaigns—Philippines—Bataan (Province)—Comic books, strips, etc. | World War, 1939–1945—Campaigns—Philippines—Corregidor Island—Comic books, strips, etc.
Classification: LCC D805.P6.B57 2022 (print) | LCC D805.P6 (ebook) | DDC 940.54/7252095991—dc23/eng/20220304
LC record available at https://lccn.loc.gov/2022005380
LC ebook record available at https://lccn.loc.gov/2022005381

Editorial Credits
Editor: Christopher Harbo; Designer: Sarah Bennett;
Production Specialist: Katy LaVigne

Design Elements
Shutterstock/Here

All internet sites appearing in back matter were available and accurate when this book was sent to press.

Direct quotations appear in bold text on the following pages:

Pages 6, 14, 20, from *We Band of Angels: The Untold Story of the American Women Trapped on Bataan* by Elizabeth M. Norman (Random House, 2011).

Page 12, from *Pure Grit: How American World War II Nurses Survived Battle and Prison Camp in the Pacific* by Mary Cronk Farrell (Harry N. Abrams, 2014).

Printed and bound in the USA. 4882

TABLE OF CONTENTS

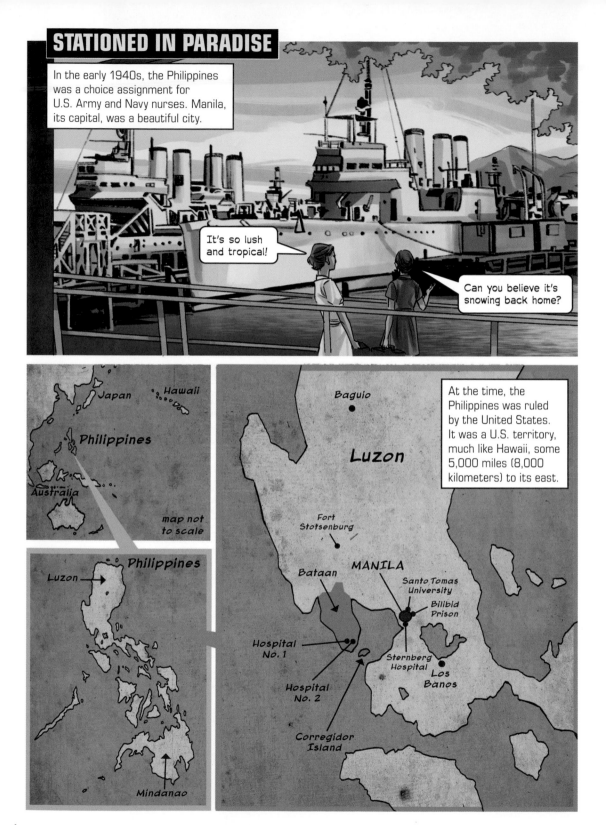

STATIONED IN PARADISE

In the early 1940s, the Philippines was a choice assignment for U.S. Army and Navy nurses. Manila, its capital, was a beautiful city.

It's so lush and tropical!

Can you believe it's snowing back home?

Japan

Hawaii

Philippines

Australia

map not to scale

Philippines

Luzon

Mindanao

Baguio

Luzon

Fort Stotsenburg

Bataan

MANILA

Santo Tomas University

Bilibid Prison

Hospital No. 1

Sternberg Hospital

Los Banos

Hospital No. 2

Corregidor Island

At the time, the Philippines was ruled by the United States. It was a U.S. territory, much like Hawaii, some 5,000 miles (8,000 kilometers) to its east.

A nurse's duties in the Philippines were light. The cases were routine at the army and navy hospitals.

Open wide.

Last one in is a rotten egg!

The nurses had a lot of free time in the tropical paradise.

Tennis, anyone?

And the nurses were thousands of miles away from the war that was troubling Europe.

Thank goodness we don't have to worry here about Hitler and his awful war.

World War II (1939–1945) had begun when Germany, led by Adolf Hitler and his Nazi party, invaded Poland. When that happened, France and Great Britain declared war on Germany. Then Japan became an ally of Germany, as did Italy.

Meanwhile, the United States didn't want to get involved in any more wars overseas. The country had endured enough horror and bloodshed fighting in World War I (1914–1918).

5

PARADISE LOST

But on December 7, 1941, Japan launched a surprise attack on the U.S. naval base at Pearl Harbor in Hawaii. More than 2,400 people were killed. Many U.S. planes and ships were destroyed.

The next day, the United States declared war on Japan.

In the early morning hours of Monday, December 8, word of the attack reached the night shift staff at U.S. Army Sternberg General Hospital in downtown Manila.

Army Nurse Lieutenant Josephine "Josie" Nesbit was in charge of the nurses that night.

What will we do?

I can't believe it!

I have friends stationed in Hawaii.

Girls, you've got to sleep today. You can't weep and wail over this, because you have to work tonight.

KABOOM!

Meanwhile, the nurses were given helmets and gas masks in case of attack.

They didn't know it, but Japanese war planes were already on the way.

About 128 miles (206 km) north of Manila, Army Nurse Ruby Bradley was sterilizing instruments at Camp John Hay Hospital in Baguio.

At 8:19 a.m., December 8, 1941, war came to the Philippines.

We're under attack!

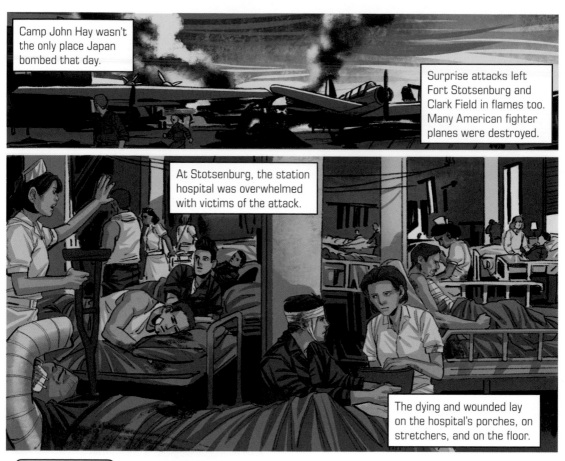

Camp John Hay wasn't the only place Japan bombed that day.

Surprise attacks left Fort Stotsenburg and Clark Field in flames too. Many American fighter planes were destroyed.

At Stotsenburg, the station hospital was overwhelmed with victims of the attack.

The dying and wounded lay on the hospital's porches, on stretchers, and on the floor.

We have to try to numb their pain.

At least this pain medication will stop them from screaming.

The nurses had no training in treating combat injuries. But they did what they could to help their patients.

Because of the bombings, the nurses at Stotsenburg were issued dog tags for the first time.

What are these for?

To identify our bodies in case we're killed.

On December 10, Japanese
warplanes attacked Manila.
They bombed Manila's port,
sinking ships and setting
the docks on fire.

St. Scholastica Girls School and other locations in Manila were quickly turned into makeshift hospitals.

One bombing raid rocked Sternberg Hospital.

It knocked Captain Maude Davison to the floor. Davison was in command of the army nurses in the Philippines.

Aaah! I've hurt my spine!

Careful, now, Captain.

With Davison injured, Lieutenant Josie Nesbit was placed in charge of the army nurses.

Since you're my deputy, you have to take over as chief nurse until I'm better.

Yes, ma'am.

In the days that followed, the horrific air attacks went on and on. The nurses did all they could to help their patients.

Quick! Move the patients under their beds to protect them from the bombs!

The nurses adapted to meet the needs of war. Their white dresses didn't work well for jumping into trenches to avoid bombs or carrying bloody stretchers.

So they were issued men's standard olive-drab coveralls. They became the first American women to wear fatigues on duty.

These fatigues are so big!

But they'll be easier to keep clean than our starched white dresses.

With the continued bombing of military bases, the army nurses at Fort Stotsenburg soon evacuated with their patients to Sternberg Hospital.

BOOM!
BOOM!
BOOM!

The bombings were soon followed by Japanese soldiers on foot. The soldiers were well-trained and well-supplied. And they were quickly approaching Manila.

The Filipino and American soldiers—who were inexperienced and outnumbered—had only one option: retreat to the Bataan Peninsula.

NURSES ON THE MOVE

Girls, pack your white duty uniforms. We're leaving tomorrow.

On December 23, 1941, the nurses were ordered to evacuate Sternberg Hospital. Some, including Davison, would go to the hospital on the island fortress of Corregidor. But most would go with the retreating forces to field hospitals on the Bataan Peninsula.

As a unit, the nurses of Bataan and Corregidor were the first large group of American women sent into combat.

They were also the first American military nurses sent onto the battlefield and the first to travel and set up hospitals in a combat area.

How am I supposed to fit all this into just one duffel bag?

Early the next morning, the first group of army nurses joined the convoy of buses and military trucks to Bataan.

So you're taking us to U.S. Army General Hospital No. 1 in Bataan, right?

Yes, ma'am.

We're here!

By evening, the nurses had finally reached their destination deep in the jungle.

This is a hospital?

I'm too tired. Let's just find our beds and get some supper.

They said the mess crew is making pancakes down at the beach.

Instead of stars in the dark night sky, they saw explosions across the bay.

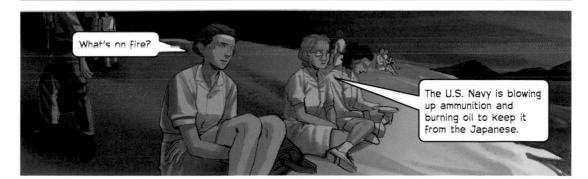

What's on fire?

The U.S. Navy is blowing up ammunition and burning oil to keep it from the Japanese.

Meanwhile, as the New Year approached, nearly two dozen nurses still remained in Manila.

Eleven of them, including Josie Nesbit, stayed at Sternberg Hospital to care for patients too injured to move. But by New Year's Eve, they too evacuated to either Bataan or Corregidor.

At the same time, 11 navy nurses still remained at the makeshift hospital at St. Scholastica. The navy nurses waited for their orders to leave too. In the chaos of war, they had been forgotten.

What's going on? The Japanese are coming. When do we leave?

Our wards are filling up with the most hopeless cases. I'm worried.

We have no orders to leave, so we stay put.

On New Year's Day, 1942, the navy nurses watched as the American flag was lowered in front of St. Scholastica.

The victorious Japanese troops marched into Manila the following day.

On January 3, Japanese officers accepted the surrender of the 27 doctors and dentists, the 11 navy nurses, a Filipino nurse, and several dozen enlisted men there.

But the nurses weren't about to let the enemy get everything.

The Japanese want to take our drugs. Let's change their names to save them for our patients.

Label this important antimalarial drug as bicarbonate of soda.

Good idea. No one will want that. Bicarbonate of soda is baking soda. You can get that anywhere.

In early March, the enemy shipped most of the remaining patients and doctors to Manila's Bilibid prison.

The 11 navy nurses were sent to Santo Tomas University across town, which the Japanese had turned into an internment camp.

JUNGLE HOSPITALS

Away from Manila, the combat on the Bataan Peninsula was intense. The American and Filipino soldiers desperately fought back Japanese attacks.

Casualties swamped Hospital No. 1 in the jungle.

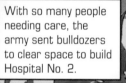

Here, let me help you.

Thank you.

The nurses worked around the clock without complaint.

With so many people needing care, the army sent bulldozers to clear space to build Hospital No. 2.

Carpenters made hospital beds, benches, and laundry baskets from the bamboo growing around them.

Medical supplies had to be carried in by soldiers along 10 miles (16 km) of narrow jungle trail.

Josie Nesbit supervised the staff at Hospital No. 2. She charged Army Nurse Sally Blaine with setting up hospital wards in the jungle.

See what you can do.

We don't have much, but at least we have a pup tent to keep the medical records dry.

But we don't have tents for our patients.

Maybe the army thinks they'll dry out faster than the records.

Blaine soon set up seven wards among the jungle paths and tangled vines. They quickly filled with patients.

Put another bed over here.

Meanwhile, Nesbit did her best to help her nurses.

Girls, I've got you some burlap. Let's section off the part of the jungle where you sleep.

We can also put up a burlap fence around a pile of rocks in the river. That way you can bathe out of sight.

We call her Mama Josie. She's always looking out for us.

She may seem stern, but she acts more like a mom than a commander.

In addition to the army nurses, she also had several Filipino nurses under her charge.

17

As the battle raged on, days stretched into weeks. Hospital No. 1 had to be moved farther south in the jungle as the fighting came too close.

We now have 2,000 patients. Some of them are even helping us out by rolling bandages.

At Hospital No. 2, Nesbit and her nurses worked around the clock.

The situation on Bataan quickly became dire. At both hospitals, an average ward of 300 patients shared six medicine glasses, 15 thermometers, and one teaspoon.

We're running out of medicine.

We're running out of everything.

People started suffering from dysentery, or bloody diarrhea. This disease was often spread through food or water contaminated by bacteria or a parasite.

Sanitation is a problem. We have only a few open pit toilets for thousands of people.

Flies from the toilets are contaminating our food and water.

Disease is striking down as many soldiers as bullets are.

Ugh! *Another* mosquito!

Jungle mosquitoes are spreading malaria. And our medical staff is getting sick too.

Food was also becoming scarce. Monkeys, lizards, and python eggs were eaten. The remaining horses and donkeys were butchered.

A lizard!

By late March, both hospitals held thousands of patients. Some were enemy soldiers captured as prisoners of war.

I don't like treating our enemies.

But I'm going to treat them as well as I'd treat a wounded American soldier.

We're nurses. That's our job.

A RETREAT AND A RESCUE

U.S. General Jonathan Wainwright was in charge of the American and Filipino soldiers on the Bataan Peninsula. He knew they couldn't withstand the constant Japanese assault. His troops were sick and starving. They had no air or artillery support. The Japanese also had a tight blockade around the peninsula to cut off supplies.

After four months of intense fighting, Wainwright knew the peninsula would have to be surrendered. On April 8, 1942, he ordered the American nurses to evacuate.

We have no choice. We have to surrender Bataan.

Have Colonel Gillespie tell the American nurses they need to evacuate to Corregidor.

Colonel Gillespie summoned Nesbit at Hospital No. 2.

Tell your American nurses to get down here by twenty hundred hours and only take whatever they can carry.

What about my Filipino nurses?

Only the American nurses.

If my Filipino nurses don't go, I'm not going either.

Gillespie respected Nesbit. He called Wainwright's headquarters.

All right. All the nurses will go.

All of the women in Nesbit's charge at Hospital No. 2 made it safely to the tiny island of Corregidor. But behind them, Bataan was falling. The troops there surrendered to the Japanese on April 9, 1942.

Now only Corregidor's island fortress was left. Soldiers manned the big guns. The marines who guarded the beach lived in dugouts and bunkers. Everyone else, some 12,000 people, lived in a complex of concrete tunnels underneath the hard rock of Malinta Hill.

The Malinta Tunnel complex was like a small, cramped city. The tunnel had been built secretly years before and had its own power and water supply.

PLAN OF MALINTA TUNNEL SYSTEM

These tunnels have dining areas, administration sections, and 1,000 hospital beds.

At Corregidor, Davison and Nesbit commanded 85 army nurses, 26 Filipino nurses, and one navy nurse, and they had their work cut out for them. With Bataan now under their control, the Japanese stepped up their bombing of Corregidor.

We're getting more casualties all the time.

I know. We've already turned the single hospital beds into bunk beds.

With so many patients, we'll have to stack the beds three high.

In the last week of April, General Wainwright was informed that two navy seaplanes would attempt to slip past the Japanese blockade and take on some passengers.

I can't rescue everyone, but give me a list of 20 of your nurses. And make sure they're ready to go.

Yes, sir.

Davison said she picked the names on her list out of a hat. But no one believed her.

Nesbit, I've put you on the list.

I know I'm older than some of the others, but I want to stay.

I can't force you to go. You can stay if that's what you really want.

It was clear she mostly chose older nurses and those who were extremely ill with tropical disease for rescue.

On the night of April 29, the planes took off with 20 nurses and other personnel.

The next morning, the seaplanes landed to refuel on one of the few Philippine Islands still in Filipino-American hands. That evening, under the cover of darkness, the planes took off again.

One plane reached the safety of Australia. But the other hit a rock beneath the waterline that ripped a hole in it.

Oh no!

Come on, we've got to get off this plane!

The passengers made it safely to land but were eventually captured by the Japanese, who had landed on the island that morning.

The men were sent to military prisons. The women were sent to work in a hospital on Mindanao until the fall. Then they were sent to the Santo Tomas Internment Camp in Manila.

On May 4, the U.S. Navy attempted another rescue on Corregidor. The submarine U.S.S. *Spearfish* floated offshore as a small boat approached with 12 American nurses, 12 military officers, and one officer's wife.

Once safely aboard, the submarine quickly sailed south to safety.

The next night, Japanese barges landed on Corregidor. On May 6, 1942, American-Filipino forces surrendered the island.

PRISONERS OF WAR

Corregidor's surrender came with a huge cost to thousands of troops, hundreds of patients, and the dozens of army nurses still on the island.

What's going to happen to us?

A group of U.S. Army women has never surrendered to an enemy before.

No matter what, we're going to uphold the highest standards of the U.S. Army Nurse Corps.

The American-Filipino troops were sent to prison in Manila. The sick and wounded would be moved to a hospital there. The nurses thought they'd go with them, but they were sent to the Santo Tomas Internment Camp instead.

No! We have to be with our patients!

We're members of the armed forces! We shouldn't be imprisoned with civilians!

Thousands of men, women, and children were held prisoner at Santo Tomas University. Most of the prisoners were American or British. The camp seemed like a small city.

Santo Tomas was governed by the Executive Committee, which was made up of prisoners under the authority of a Japanese commandant. The Executive Committee was given a small amount of money to buy food for the prisoners.

The Executive Committee organized a school for the children. There were language classes, a library, and even a 16-piece orchestra.

The prisoners played cards, put on plays, and formed a baseball league. They also had small plots where they could try to grow food.

The 11 navy nurses from St. Scholastica had converted the university machine shop into a small hospital. It was staffed with civilian doctors and other captured nurses.

But the camp was still a prison. If anyone tried to escape, they would be beaten or shot.

At Santo Tomas, Davison established discipline and military routine over the nurses. With more prisoners coming in, she also organized a larger camp hospital. The nurses reported there every day to care for patients.

We're still members of the United States Army Nurse Corps, even if we're prisoners of war.

Our first duty is to take care of our patients, no matter what.

Then, in early September, the nurses were surprised by a new group of prisoners. The 10 nurses who had been evacuated by seaplane at Corregidor arrived at Santo Tomas.

Our plane got damaged--it couldn't take off. Then we got captured by the Japanese.

At least you're alive!

Every day, more and more prisoners arrived. The camp became so crowded that in May 1943, the Japanese set up another internment camp near the town of Los Banos.

Eleven navy nurses and 800 men left for the new camp. But three days later, 800 more internees arrived at Santo Tomas. There were also almost 200 children under the age of five.

In early 1944, the Japanese commandant left Santo Tomas, and the Japanese military took control of the camp. They cut off supplies of medicine.

Nurses had fewer ways to treat their patients, but they still had to care for them no matter what.

We will also no longer give money for food. We will provide the food for you.

Rations were cut and then cut again. Soon the camp was starving. Children dug through garbage cans for scraps at the Japanese army mess hall.

People ate anything they could find, including stray cats, sparrows, and rats.

I found some weeds to eat. I'm going to fry them in sour cream.

Can I have some?

By the end of January 1945, as many as five people a day starved to death. The camp was now surviving on one meal every day—usually a cup of vegetable gruel.

A camp survey showed that on average, male internees had lost 51 pounds (23 kilograms). The women had lost 32 pounds (15 kg).

Here, try to drink a little water.

But every day, the nurses, ill and starving, reported to work. Caring for others gave them a mission and kept them alive.

It's our boys!

The situation was desperate, but the Philippines were not forgotten. Prisoners had seen American fighter planes flying a raid across Manila.

Then, on February 3, 1945, the nurses heard the sounds of gunfire and explosions across the city. A formation of U.S. planes soon flew low over the camp.

They're finally coming to rescue us!

ROLL OUT THE BARREL
SANTA CLAUS IS COMING
SUNDAY OR MONDAY

Hooray!

The nurses' long ordeal at Santo Tomas was finally over.

The navy nurses, who had been moved to Los Banos Internment Camp in May 1943, were freed three weeks later.

Unbelievably, all of the army and navy nurses of Bataan and Corregidor survived, including the prisoners of war.

These women had no combat or survival training. Yet through their shared work and sense of purpose, they survived the harshest conditions imaginable.

Upon their release, the nurses were promoted. They got medals, gave press interviews, and had ticker-tape parades.

And then they were largely forgotten.

But not by the men who survived Bataan and Corregidor.

On April 9, 1980, they erected a plaque in the nurses' honor on the Bataan Peninsula. In doing so, they hoped that no one would ever forget that these heroic women had "truly earned the name—the Angels of Bataan and Corregidor."

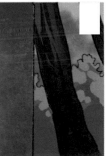

TO THE ANGELS

GLOSSARY

artillery (ar-TIL-uh-ree)—cannons and other large guns used during battles

blockade (blok-AYD)—a military effort to keep goods from entering and leaving a region

bunker (BUHNG-kuhr)—an underground shelter from bomb attacks and gunfire

commandant (KAA-muhn-daant)—a commanding officer of a place or group

convoy (KON-voi)—a group of vehicles traveling together, usually accompanied by armed forces

dysentery (DI-sen-tayr-ee)—a serious infection of the intestines that can be deadly; dysentery is often caused by drinking contaminated water

evacuate (i-VA-kyuh-wayt)—to leave a dangerous place to go somewhere safer

fatigues (fuh-TEEGS)—a soldier's work clothing

internee (in-tuhr-NEE)—a person who is forced to live at an internment camp

internment camp (in-TURN-muhnt CAMP)—a prison camp for prisoners of war

malaria (muh-LAIR-ee-ah)—a serious disease that people get from mosquito bites; malaria causes high fever, chills, and sometimes death

peninsula (puh-NIN-suh-luh)—a piece of land that is surrounded by water on three sides

ration (RASH-uhn)—a daily share of food

sterilize (STER-uh-lize)—to clean something so thoroughly that no germs or dirt remain

READ MORE

Serrano, Christy. *The Attack on Pearl Harbor: A Day that Changed America.* North Mankato, MN: Capstone, 2022.

Taylor, Susan. *Women in World War Two.* New York: Children's Press, 2021.

Tyner, Artika R. *The Courageous Six Triple Eight: The All-Black Female Battalion of World War II.* North Mankato, MN: Capstone, 2023.

INTERNET SITES

The Angels of Bataan: The World War II Nurses Who Survived Three Years in a Japanese Prison Camp amightygirl.com/blog?p=24228

Captured Army Nurses: The Philippines—World War II history.army.mil/html/topics/women/captured nurses.html

Nurse POWs: Angels of Bataan and Corregidor nationalww2museum.org/war/articles/nurse-pows-bataan-and-corregidor

ABOUT THE AUTHOR

Photo credit:
Agnieszka Biskup

Agnieszka Biskup is a writer and editor who lives in Chicago. She was an editor at the *Boston Globe* newspaper and studied science journalism at MIT. Agnieszka was also the managing editor of the children's magazine *Muse*. She has written many children's books, as well as articles for newspapers, magazines, and the web. Her books have won many awards, including an American Institute of Physics Science Writing Award, where instead of a trophy, she got a chair. (Yes, the kind you sit in. It is very nice.)

ABOUT THE ILLUSTRATOR

Photo credit: Muso

Samantha F. Chow is an Indonesian illustrator currently based on the beautiful island of Bali. She studied film and game art design in Malaysia, and later completed her illustration degree in London. Sam enjoys drawing stories, everyday life, and anything historical! Being a curious person, Sam also loves to travel, exploring new places while doodling her journeys in her handy little sketchbooks!